How to Write a Will

An Easy To Follow Guide To Writing Your Own Legal Will (Including Templates!)

1st Edition

Written By Daniel Hughes

© **Copyright 2017 by Daniel Hughes - All rights reserved.**

This document is geared towards providing exact and reliable information in regards to the topic and issue covered. The publication is sold with the idea that the publisher is not required to render accounting, officially permitted, or otherwise, qualified services. If advice is necessary, legal or professional, a practiced individual in the profession should be ordered.

- From a Declaration of Principles which was accepted and approved equally by a Committee of the American Bar Association and a Committee of Publishers and Associations.

In no way is it legal to reproduce, duplicate, or transmit any part of this document in either electronic means or in printed format. Recording of this publication is strictly prohibited and any storage of this document is not allowed unless with written permission from the publisher. All rights reserved.

The information provided herein is stated to be truthful and consistent, in that any liability, in terms of inattention or otherwise, by any usage or abuse of any policies, processes, or directions contained within is the solitary and utter responsibility of the recipient reader. Under no circumstances will any legal responsibility or blame be held against the publisher for any reparation, damages, or monetary loss due to the information herein, either directly or indirectly.

Respective authors own all copyrights not held by the publisher.

The information herein is offered for informational purposes solely, and is universal as so. The presentation of the information is without contract or any type of guarantee assurance.

The trademarks that are used are without any consent, and the publication of the trademark is without permission or backing by the trademark owner. All trademarks and brands within this book are for clarifying purposes only and are the owned by the owners themselves, not affiliated with this document.

Table of Contents

Introduction 1
Chapter 1 – The Importance of a Will 3
    Understanding Succession 3
        Intestate Succession versus Testamentary Succession 3
    Definition of a Will 5
    Characteristics of a Will...................................... 5
    Limitations of a Will 10
    Parties to a Will.. 16
Chapter 2 – Executing a Will 17
    Importance of Executing a Will......................... 17
    Who can execute a will?..................................... 20
        Legal Capacity to Execute 20
Kinds of Wills 23
    Oral Wills.. 23
    Written Wills 23
Chapter 3 – Formalities of Written Wills.............. 25
    Requirements of a Valid Will 25
        Essential or Necessary Requirements........... 25
        Extrinsic or Formal Requirements of a Will 28

Chapter Four: Specific Formalities of Different Type of Wills 33

Formalities of Holographic Wills 33

Examples of Holographic Will 36

Formalities of Formal Will 40

Example of a Formal Will 45

Chapter Five: Writing Testamentary Dispositions 52

Disposing Properties in Your Will 52

Properties that Can Be Disposed 54

Granting and Revoking Rights 57

Rights that can be Granted in the Will 58

Rights that can be Revoked in the Will 59

Disinheriting an Heir 60

Disposing Obligations 62

Pure Oligation 62

Conditional Obligations 63

Chapter 6: Revocation, Destruction and Execution of the Will 68

Disposing the Property Subject of the Will 68

Revocation of the Will 68

Destruction of the Will 70

Codicils and Altering the Original Will without Making a New One 70

Validity of Codicil 70

>   Execution of the Will 71
>
>>   Probate of the Will... 72
>>
>>   Who Can Bring the Will for Probate? 73
>>
>>   Effect if the Will is Declared Invalid by the Probate Court 73
>
> Conclusion... 74

Introduction

Thank you for purchasing this book "How to Write a Will: An Easy to Follow Guide to Writing Your Own Legal Will (Including Templates!)".

Many people think that having or writing a will is only for rich people. Some are hesitant to have a legal will because they believed that they do not have any property to give or bequeath.

However, a legal will is not only for the rich or for those with many properties to bestow. It is an important part of a civilized society. The writing of wills had been observed over 2000 years ago. It had established empires and countries and prevented wars in many states. The nobility observed writing of wills to prevent bloodshed in the issue of succession.

A person's will becomes his most precious possession and superior orders. No one can go against it, unless the terms are against the law or the testator did not have the authority to order it.

Writing a will is a vital part of civilization that almost every state has a law governing the making, validity and the execution of the will. This made writing a will complicated. It discouraged simple people from leaving a will.

Writing a will is actually simple. It only seems complicated because many lawyers make it look complex, so you would engage their services. The truth, however, is that the laws used in most states adhere to basic international laws. These laws are far simpler than national or local laws that even a high school student could understand.

This book teaches you all that you need to know about Wills and how to write one of your own. It would mention international laws that might affect the form and validity of your will. Do not be intimidated or discouraged. This book explains it in a way you would understand it, without a need of consulting a lawyer.

This is a complete walkthrough that would lead you to understanding and being able to write a valid legal will. It will not only save you legal fees, but you can command your will precisely how you want it.

This book does not only teach you about how to write a will, but it also teaches you your rights as an heir, too.

I hope you would learn many from this book.

Chapter 1 – The Importance of a Will

Understanding Succession

Succession is one way of acquiring a property, rights or obligation from another person upon his death.

The rules on succession are the basis of the validity of the provisions in a will or the will itself. Thus, it is important to understand succession first, before you prepare a will.

There are two kinds of succession. These are intestate succession and testamentary succession.

Intestate Succession versus Testamentary Succession

These two types of succession are mostly differentiated by the existence of a will.

Intestate Succession

Intestate succession takes place when the person died without leaving any will or the will he left is void.

In this type of succession, the law controls how the properties, rights, and obligation of a person should be distributed among his legal heirs. The law also declares who the heir or heirs should be.

It is common in intestate succession that the nearest degree descendants become the legal heir and in the absence thereof, the ascendants. If none exist, then the nearest kin would become the legal heir. This is regardless of how the decedent felt about him.

For example: Sam died leaving three children. His children would automatically become his heirs. They would partition his estate equally among themselves.

Let's assume that Sam despised his third child, Ben, and would not have let the latter receive any inheritance. If Sam died without a will, Ben could still inherit Sam's properties.

Testamentary Succession

When a valid will is made by the decedent, the succession becomes a testamentary succession. This means that the decedent, which also now becomes the testator, is controlling how his properties, rights and obligation will be distributed upon his death, but in a manner provided and limited by law.

The decedent is allowed to institute his heir or heirs. He can impose conditions when giving his properties. He can also appoint trustees or administrators for his property, for the protection of another person or his minor children. Filiation and kinship may also be established by the testator through a will. He could also disinherit a child or a possible heir.

Definition of a Will

In many states, a will is defined as an act whereby a person can give or dispose his properties, obligations and rights, but the disposal would only be effective upon his death and if permitted by the law.

Characteristics of a Will

A Will is an Act

Many people think that a will is a document, prepared by the deceased and narrating what he wished to give, bestow and bequeath to other people. This is not what a will is.

A will is actually the act of giving, bestowing, and bequeathing your estate upon your death. It may, in some instances, allow you to demand, revoke and oblige other people to do something for your estate or for your desires.

It does not have to be written. A person can express his will other than by writing. He can leave his will through another person, or record it through other media.

However, many states only recognize written wills and testaments. Hence, the assumption that a will is a written document became more acceptable.

A Will Can Give and Dispose Properties, Rights and Obligations

Another misconception about a will is that it only bestows intangible or tangible properties. A will has purposes other than bestowing properties. It can also give obligations and rights, even after his death.

- Giving Properties

This is the most common provision in the will. The provision usually starts with "I give and bequeath".

Let's assume that Ben wrote in his will that, "I give and bequeath my mansion to Sam."

Upon Ben's death, Sam would get the mansion.

- Bestowing a Right

As said before, a will is a superior act of the decedent. Disrespecting it would be a violation of a law. No person can bend or ignore the legal will of a person unless it is against the law. Thus, when a person gives a right to a person in his will, that person might be entitled to that right.

A good example of this is the acknowledgement of a filial relationship. For example, Sam is an illegitimate child of Ben. He was never acknowledged by Ben, while the latter was alive. However, on his last will, Ben acknowledged that Sam is his child.

This act would bestow upon Sam all the necessary and implied rights an illegitimate child may have from his father. Now, no one may contest this right from Sam, except if he questions it himself or if there is a local or national law revoking such will.

Other examples would be giving a person the right to be a tenant in his property for a period allowed by the federal or state law.

- Giving Obligation

There are instances that a will may not dispose properties or rights, but would give an obligation to a person. The obligation may be absolute or conditional. However, the obligation must be something the testator can demand or give.

Example of an Absolute Obligation Provision

Sam wrote in his will, "I hereby demand Ben to pay me $3000, which I loaned to him on May 22, 2017."

If Ben had not paid Sam during the latter's lifetime, the will becomes a rightful act of demand against Ben. The obligation would be invalid if Ben could prove that he already paid the loan, while Sam was alive.

Now, you might wonder what happens if Ben pays the $3000 after the execution of the will. The money becomes part of Sam's estate and whoever is the instituted heir or heirs, gets that money.

Example of a Conditional Obligation Provision

In this situation, the subject of the provision has an option whether to accept or not the condition. The obligation is often anchored to a right that may only be bestowed after the condition is perfected or executed.

For example: Sam declares in his will that Ben would become the owner of his car, if Ben acknowledges that he is the better bowler.

If Ben accepts the condition, then he earns the right to become the owner of the car. However, if he refuses, then he earns no right. Sam or the executioner of the will does not have the right to force him to accept.

You might wonder what would happen to the car if Ben refuses to accept the condition. It will revert back to the estate of the decedent and will be distributed to his legal or instituted heirs.

- *A will is a personal act*

The making of a will and the provisions included therein should be the personal act of the testator. A will that was written or executed under undue influence, force and intimidation is often deemed void. However, the influence, force, and intimidation should be something grave that the testator could not resist.

All the dispositions in the will should be based on the benevolence and/or voluntary acts of the testator.

For example: Ben forced Sam to execute a will, instituting Ben as his sole heir. Ben threatened to kill Sam's family if he refused. If Sam died, the will would be deemed void.

However, if Ben's threat is only to deprive Sam access to the fitness gym, the will may still be deemed valid.

Limitations of a Will

A person can write any disposition of properties, bestow any right, or demand conditions in his will. However, his provision or the whole will may be subject to limitation. Here are some of the limitations:

- The person should have the right over the properties he gave, owns the right, he wishes to bestow, and the right to demand;

- The person should be permitted by the law of his state or country of nationality.

- *The person should have the right over the properties he gave*

A person could only give what he owns. Even if it is true that a will should be respected, it would not be given effect if the decedent does not have the rights over the properties, rights, and obligation in his will.

For example, Sam gives and bequeaths his neighbour's house to his best friend, Ben.

Ben could not demand Sam's neighbour to give him the house to honour Sam's will. This provision would prejudice the real owner of the house and thus, should not be honoured. In fact, in some states, the will would automatically be declared void because the testator obviously makes a joke out of his will.

- *The decedent should have the right to bestow a right*

A majority of countries allows a person to waive or bestow his rights. However, the person could only do so if he is entitled to that right or allowed to waive that right. A will is not an exception to this limitation.

To illustrate: Sam acknowledges Ben to be his long lost brother, but his parents or legal heir presented an essential evidence to prove that they are not siblings, either by affinity, or consanguinity.

The State or any person would not be obliged to acknowledge Ben as Sam's brother to honour the latter's last will. The logic of this limitation is to disallow other people to abuse the decedent and to rob other legal heirs of their rights.

- *The decedent should have the right to demand*

A person can only demand something if he is entitled to it. Thus, unless the decedent has the right to demand, he cannot oblige any person to do something in his will.

For example: Sam demands Ben pay the college tuition of Sam's son. Ben does not owe anything to Sam. The latter did not entrust any money to Ben for the college tuition. Thus, Sam's son could not demand Ben to fulfil Sam's provision.

- *The person should be permitted by the law of his state or by his country of nationality*

As they say, even in death, you would not have absolute freedom. A person's last will is still subject to the laws and formalities required by the law.

There are many common instances where a will is deemed void or could not be executed because of conflicts with the law. Each country may prescribe different limitations to the decedent. Here are some instances that could limit a person's disposition on his will or could declare his will void:

1. *The existence of compulsory heirs.*
   Many states give precedence to compulsory heirs. A portion of the decedent's estates is often reserved for them.

   Compulsory heirs are usually the descendants or ascendants of the decedent. These are his legitimate children, or in the absence thereof, his parents. In some cases, illegitimate children are also considered compulsory heirs.

   The states usually protect compulsory heirs in order to preserve family ties.

For example: Sam has an estate worth $200,000. He has two children, Eric and James. There is a law stating that half of the decedent's estate should be reserved for his compulsory heirs. If Sam wrote in his will that he gives and bequeaths all his estate to Ben, the provision or the will may not be honoured because it violates the law.

Such violation is known as preterition. It is a ground to declare the will void in many countries.

2. *The responsibility of the decedent to pay taxes*
Taxes are the source of income for every nation. It is always given a priority in almost transactions, even in the distribution of the decedent's estate.

The usual rule in most states is that the estate tax should be paid before the will can be validly executed. If the estate could not cover all the dispositions in the will, some of the provisions may not be honoured.

To illustrate: Sam has an estate of $100,000. He owes the government taxes for $30,000.

In his will he provided to leave all his estate to Ben.

Ben would not receive the whole estate. He will only get what is left after the tax was deducted.

3. *The obligation of the decedent to provide for his minor children.*

The will may be declared void or some of the provisions would be dishonoured if the testator fails to reserve sufficient amount in his estate to support his minor children.

Let's say, Sam has four minor children. He has an estate of $100,000, which he left solely to Ben. If this provision will be honoured, Sam's children would be prejudice. Further, the state will also be prejudiced because they would have to support Sam's children.

Thus, Sam's will may be dishonoured by the State or the latter may cause his will to be modified.

This act of the State would be in accordance with the long observe doctrine of *parens Patriae,* which designates the State as the legal protector and guardian of his people.

Parties to a Will

The following people are the parties to a will:

1. *The testator or the decedent.* He makes the will and disposes his properties.

2. *The instituted heir.* The instituted heir or heirs are the beneficiary of all the remaining estate after the disposition. However, they may also receive properties, rights or obligation through testamentary disposition.

Example: Sam instituted Ben as his heir. He bequeathed his properties. Most of them were given to Ben. After all the dispositions were executed, Sam still had $20,000.

If there are no limitations on compulsory heirs, Ben would get that $20,000.

3. *Legatee.* A legatee is an heir who receives personal properties, whether tangible or intangible.

If Ben is to receive cars from Sam, he shall be referred to as the legatee.

4. *Devisee.* This is an heir who receives real estate properties.

If Ben is to receive an apartment in Bel-Air, then he can be referred to as the devisee.

Chapter 2 – Executing a Will

The Importance of Executing a Will

A will may not be necessary, but it is an advantage to prepare one. Here are some of the reasons to prepare a will:

1. *It prevents family disputes over your estate.*

Succession would refer to order of things. However, if a person dies intestate, the order of things may not be established. This can cause conflicts among the heirs, and may result to loss of properties.

To illustrate: Sam died intestate leaving three sons and a multi-million family business. His three sons would inherit his business equally, as may be provided by the basic inheritance law. The children could have equal amount of shares. However, there would be a question as to who will become the head of the business.

This situation may force the siblings to sue or fight each other. If they fail to reach a settlement, the usual remedy is to sell the property and they divide the proceeds among themselves.

However, if Sam left a will and designated one of his sons to be the chairman or created a scheme for the transfer of chairmanship, then his children would be forced to follow that provision.

Written wills are the most accepted type of wills in most states. A written will can be formal or holographic.

2. *You can continue to protect the persons you want to protect.*

Intestate succession may deprive some people you love the right to inherit from you. Thus, they are left unprotected and with no inheritance to support them. However, these people may be protected if you provide some protection for them in your will.

For example: Ben, one of Sam's sons is an illegitimate child. Many states do not allow an illegitimate child to inherit under intestate succession. Therefore, Ben could not inherit from Sam, even if it would have been obvious that the latter would have wanted Ben to have a portion of his fortune.

However, if Sam clearly bequeathed 1/3 of his fortune to Ben, the latter would be entitled to that portion, even if the law prohibits an illegitimate child to inherit under intestate proceedings.

Another situation would be the assignment of a legal guardian to your minor children and administrator to your properties.

3. You can make a confession or acknowledge something, which you cannot do so during your lifetime.

Many countries regard the will to be a "dying declaration" of a testator. Everything that is provided therein should be assumed to be true, unless proven otherwise.

If a testator acknowledges a person to be his descendant, the same would be accepted as true until it is proven otherwise.

Also, if a testator narrates in his will a crime he committed or witnessed, the same may be used as evidence. The logic of this is based on the assumption that a person would not lie while facing his impending death.

4. You can continue to fulfil your obligations even after you are dead.

Some obligations may be extinguished when you die. However, if you choose to continue the fulfilment of the obligation, you may provide it through your will.

For example: Sam promised to buy Ben's mansion on December 25, 2018, but he found out that he is dying. He could leave a provision on his will to continue the purchase of Ben's mansion.

The other heirs may not question it because the mansion would still become part of Sam's estate.

Who can execute a will?

Any person can execute a will provided that:

1. He has the legal capacity and/or of legal age; and
2. He was of sound mind when he made the will;

Legal Capacity to Execute

A person should have the capacity under the law to execute a will. It is assume that a person acquires legal capacity to execute a will when he reaches the legal age, unless a law provides a different age.

The legal capacity only affects the right to execute, but not the right to receive any of the estate of the deceased. So, a testator can institute a minor as his heir, devisee, or legatee.

Soundness of Mind

A testator is required to be of sound mind when he executes a will. This is to ensure that he understood the implications of the provisions on the instrument. It is also to prevent other people from abusing a person of unsound mind.

Note that the requirement of soundness of mind is only required during the making of the will. If the testator becomes insane or incapacitated after he made the will, his subsequent incapacity will not affect the validity of his will.

As a general rule, everyone is deemed of sound mind unless it is proven otherwise.

Deaf-Mutes and Blind Testator

Deaf-mutes and blind people can still make their own will, provided they comply with two general requisites.

If the testator is deaf-mute or only deaf, he should be allowed to read his will before signing.

A blind testator can only make formal wills because he is required to have the will read to him according to the number of witnesses.

Who can be an heir, legacy, or devisee?

There is no limit as to who can be the heir, legacy or devisee. The testator can give, bestow or oblige anyone whom he wishes to. However, the heir, legacy or devisee may have to meet the requirement set forth by the state before they could receive what was given to them.

> For example:
>
> Ben, a Filipino Citizen, gave Sam, an American Citizen, 3000 acres of land, which he owned in the Philippines. However, the constitution of the Philippines prohibits an alien to own a real estate in the Philippines.
>
> In this case, Sam may not be able to receive the property because the same may not be executed.

A minor can be an heir, provided, that a legal guardian would be assigned to them. The legal guardian can be nominated by the testator itself, or be assigned by the Probate Court during the probate proceeding.

Kinds of Wills

There are two types of wills in general. These are the Oral Wills and the Written Wills.

Oral Wills

Many countries had stopped recognizing oral wills because it is difficult to prove that what the testimony of the witness is the will of the testator. However, due to the development of times, oral wills are slowly accepted in some states, provided that it is video-taped and the testator expressed his intention to make it as his last will and testament.

Written Wills

Written wills are the more recognized around the world because they are more tangible. The provisions on the will can easily be assumed as the intention of the testator because it might be written with his own handwriting, witnessed or notarized.

There are two general types of written wills – the holographic will and the formal will.

- Holographic Will

A holographic will is one that is entirely handwritten by the decedent. It is the most personal, easiest, and cheapest way of making a will. It does not need to conform with any form, provided that it is dated and signed.

It can be a simple letter giving and bequeathing properties, rights and obligations to the heirs.

However, holographic wills are often protested. The usual ground is the verification of the handwriting – whether it is the testators or not. The procedure of countering the protest can become expensive. The heirs named in the will may have to hire an expert to prove the handwriting, since there are no witnesses during the will was made.

- Formal Will

Formal will can be handwritten or typewritten. It is signed and dated by the testator before the required number of witnesses and/or before a notary public or solicitor. A will prepared by a notary public is often called a notarial will.

Experts recommend the making of formal will, instead of holographic will. Formal wills are stronger because it is attested by witnesses that should not be an heir, recipient, devisee or legatee of the testator.

A holographic will may also become a formal will if the testator would have it attested by witnesses.

Notarial will, on the other hand, is more preferred by many. It is less challenged because it is prepared by lawyers or solicitors. Thus, in many countries, notarial wills do not have to be probated by the state.

Chapter 3 – Formalities of Written Wills

A will is always valid. This is the general rule and an accepted principle in International law. If no one objects to the will, the same would be executed according to the dispositions provided therein. States and courts of law would grant the testators wish, as much as possible.

Requirements of a Valid Will
A will have two requirements. These are the essential requirements and the formal requirements.

Essential or Necessary Requirements
The essential or necessary requirements are those that give effects to the will. The omission of such requirements would invalidate the whole will and turn it into a piece of blank paper.

Below are the necessary requirements for a will to be valid:

1. Name or description of the testator;
2. Signature of the testator;
3. Date;
4. Valid testamentary dispositions;

5. Witnesses to the will if the will is a formal will;
6. Declaration of Non-Preterition

- **Name or Description of the Testator**

Though the name may not be as important as the signature, it is still a necessary requirement for a will. The testator must first be identified before the execution of his will and the best way to identify the testator is through his name.

There are instances that the testator may or forgotten to put down his name. This omission may not immediately declare the will void, if it had enough description of the testator to establish his identity and a signature to back it up. This is common to holographic will.

For example: Steve Jobs did not place his name in his will, but he mentioned in his will that he is the founder of Apple. Since the whole world knows that he is the founder of apple, the will would easily be identified as his. But, it has to be confirmed by his signature.

- **Signature of the Testator**

The signature confirms the willingness of the testator to make the will and that all provisions therein were true to his intentions. In some cases, it is also a confirmation of the testator's identity.

The signature required may depend on the kind of will. The real or the common signature of the testator is preferred in many cases.

However, there are instances that a simple "x" or a thumb mark may be accepted, especially if the testator was physically incapacitated when the will was made. This is only recognized in formal wills.

- **Date**

The date is as important as the signature. Unless and until the testator places the date, the last will and testament will have no effect. It is also a confirmation that the testator intended the will to be his last will and testament.

A date placed after the testator is dead would not cure the defect.

The date must be complete. If the testator refused to place a complete date in his will, it only shows his intention not to make the will effective.

A date does not have to be in calendar form. Dates such as "New Year's Eve, 2017", "Valentine's Day,

2012" or "Christmas Day, 2005, are considered valid dates for a will.

- **Valid Testamentary Dispositions**

The will must have valid testamentary dispositions. A defective testamentary disposition may not declare the will inoperative, but there are some testamentary dispositions that could do so.

In Chapter 5, this book will discuss thoroughly about testamentary disposition.

- **Witnesses to the Will**

Witnesses to the will are essential for formal wills. Formal wills give lesser emphasis to the identity of the testator. There would be entries about the testator's identity that may be entered incorrectly because it is made by another person. The intentions of the testator may be distorted. The purpose of the witness is to attest that the will was affirmed and accepted by the testator by signing his name.

Extrinsic or Formal Requirements of a Will

The will needs to comply with formal requirements in order to be complete. Omission of the formal requirements may not make your will invalid, but it might render a provision ineffective or vague.

Unlike the intrinsic requirements, the defect in the extrinsic requirements may be cured

Some of the formal requirements are:

1. *Citizenship*

You should indicate your citizenship and/or nationality in your will. The testamentary succession of a person usually follows the law of the land, where he is a citizen or a national. It is not where he died or where his properties are located.

Question: Sam is a Californian Citizen. He executed a will in Paris, France and died in Moscow, Russia. Now, what law should govern his will?

Answer: The California Law on Succession. However, if the Californian law declares that the testamentary succession should follow the law where the will was made, then the law of succession of France would be followed.

The citizenship of the heirs, legatee or devisee must also be indicated. This is to determine whether they may be allowed to accept the inheritance.

2. *The description of the property you are bequeathing.*

You should describe the property you are giving to your heir. You should include their exact location and their general structure. This is to avoid confusion.

For example: Sam has two mansions in Orange County. He devised one of them to his son, Ben, but he did not describe which of the two mansions Ben should get.

The will may still be valid, but the disposition may be dishonored for being vague.

3. *The description of the person or the name of the person, who is your heir, legatee or devisee.*

A testator can put the real name of the person who is his heir, legatee or devisee. The testator also has the option not to indicate the name, but indicate the description of the person, instead.

Thus, when the testator leaves a portion of his estate to a friend who has one leg and brown eyes, the said provision would still be valid.

The description is more important than the name, especially if two or more persons have the same name.

- Curing the Defective Extrinsic Requirements

The defects on the extrinsic requirements of a will may be cured by the following:

1. Agreement by the heirs;
2. Testimony of the witness or witnesses;
3. Declaration of the probate or Inheritance courts;

A. Agreement by the Heirs

The heirs could amicably settle the defect to avoid legal disputes. This is the most practical way. The will and the testamentary dispositions would still be valid, but the execution thereof may be delayed if the heirs refuse to cure the defect on their own.

For example:

Sam gives and bequeaths $10,000 to his favorite student, Ben Jones. There are two Ben Jones in his class. Now, who would get it?

The two Ben Jones could agree to split the inheritance, instead of proving that only one of them is the favorite student.

B. By the Testimony of the Witness

The confusion because of a defect in the extrinsic requirement can easily be cured by a witness to the will. The testimony of witness to the will would have a superior weight. His declaration may be as good as the declaration of the probate or inheritance courts.

To illustrate using the same example in the preceding paragraph:

Timothy James attested that Sam referred to Ben Jones, a student he coached in a chess tournament. Therefore, the whole $10,000 would be awarded to the specified Ben Jones.

C. By Declaration of Probate or Inheritance Court

A drastic option for the heirs to cure an extrinsic defect is to file a proceeding in the court of law. They may need to present witnesses and evidence to prove that the intent of the testator.

However, this option opens the will of the testator to further questions. There are instances that the probate court may declare the whole will void because it found a substantive defect on the will.

Chapter Four: Specific Formalities of Different Type of Wills

Different types of Wills may require other formalities to make them valid. Below shows the specific requirements for two types of written will:

Formalities of Holographic Wills

1. *The language should be one that is spoken or understood by the testator.*

It is to prove that the latter was not forced or influenced in making his will. Also, it is to avoid misinterpretation of the dispositions in the will.

> Example: Ben is Chinese and he barely speaks and understands English. If he wrote a holographic will in English, others may become suspicious about how he could make it.

2. *Everything should be entirely in the handwriting of the testator. If any line in the holographic will is written by another person, the will might become null and void.*

A holographic will should remain a secret until the testator's death. Any sign that it was altered by another person could invalidate the whole will, regardless whether the testator signed and dated the alteration or cause the alteration.

> For example: Ben wrote a holographic will and entrusted Sam to be the executor. Sam noticed that the will was not dated. When he told Ben about it, Ben ordered him to write the date himself.
>
> This simple alteration would make Ben's will null and void.

3. The testator should sign it in his most common signature. He should not make a separate or new signature for his will. It may not make the will invalid, but it can raise doubts.

The best proof of the identity of the testator in a holographic will is his signature. A slight doubt in his signature may make the will questionable.

If the testator has two or more signatures, any of the signatures can be accepted.

4. Any additions, erasures, revisions should be signed and dated;

Additions, erasures, revisions not signed and dated would not nullify he will. However, the addition, erasures, revisions would not be honored. In some cases, an alteration that is in conflict with the original intention of the testator may be a ground to declare the will invalid.

5. If the will exceeds one page, the testator should sign and date every page. Also, he should write the page numbers.

A testator should sign and date each page of his holographic will. If he fails to do so, the provisions on the unsigned and undated page would not be honored. This is to prevent others from altering a few of the pages of the will.

6. The testator should make it clear that he intends to leave the instrument as his will.

A holographic will may not follow the forms of notarial or formal will. The testator could write the will in a letter form or in any other form, provided, that he clearly states his intention to make it as his will.

Examples of Holographic Will

A. Holographic Will similar to Formal Will

My Last Will and Testament

I, Sam Davis, a resident of Oakley, California, of legal age, and of sound mind, hereby declare this instrument to be my last will and testament. The dispositions listed herein are of my voluntary act and will and they are as follows:

I hereby declare that upon my death, I want to be buried in a tomb next to my late wife.

To my daughter, Ana, I give and bequeath my property, a house and lot, located in Mission District, San Francisco, California. However, I impose a condition that the said property shall not be sold within five years upon my death.

To my son, Alex, I give and bequeath all the cars and vehicles under my name at the time of my death and $200,000 worth of shares from my company, SS Holding.

To my son Ben, who I officially institute as my heir, I hereby give and bequeath all other properties and rights under my name at the time of my death.

I direct my friend, Thomas, an American Citizen, of legal age and a resident of Mission District, San Francisco, California as the legal executor of this will.

I hereby declare that I have not executed any other will, except for this one.

Signed this 25th day of May, 2017.

Signature

Sam Davis

B. Letter Form of Holographic Will

May 25, 2017

Dear Ben,

My time in this life is about to end. I feel like I should settle things with you and your siblings, so you would not fight over my estate. Son, when I die, make sure to do everything I wish in this letter. This will be my last will and testament.

1. *Give this house to your sister, Ann.*

2. *Give $200,000 to Alex, which he should solely use for putting up the restaurant business he wished.*

As for you, I give you all the cars and my stocks in SS Holdings. If there are still properties left, I want you to divide it equally among you and your siblings.

Also, make sure to give Mr. Thomas the amount of $10,000, to be taken from my estate, as my gratitude for his loyalty for more than 10 years.

I wish that you and your siblings will continue to love and care for each other even if after I am gone.

Love,

Your Father

*This will may not bear the name of the testator. The words "your father" is already sufficient to establish his identity and the heirs.

- ➢ The will is valid even if it is in the letter form because the testator clearly expressed his intention to make it his last will and testament. Writing it directly to his son, Ben, is tantamount to assigning Ben as the executor of his will.

C. Examples of Holographic Wills that May be Deemed Invalid or Nullified

May 25, 2017

Dear Ben,

I was hit by a car yesterday. I thought I would die, but luckily I survived. While I was in the hospital, I thought about what to do with my cars. There are eight of them. Thomas loves most of them.

It would be great if he will have all of them after I die. I know that you would be very happy.

I also thought of my son, Alex. As you know, he is an illegitimate child and I cannot give him a lot. I want to give him at least $200,000 just to let him start his own business and be secured in the future.

I don't care about my other properties. I guess, my other children could divide them among themselves.

Let's have lunch when you come back. I really want to spend more time with you. We don't know when death would take us.

Your friend,

Sam Davis

- This letter would not be accepted as a holographic will because there was no clear intention for the writer that he wished it to be his last will. The letter is merely a friendly communication.

Thus, even if there were testamentary dispositions and acknowledgement of right in the letter, the same would not be honored.

Formalities of Formal Will

Some of the formalities of a formal will or notarial will are the same with the notarial will. However, third persons are given rights, in some extent, to participate in the making of the will.

Below are the formalities of a formal will:

1. *It must be attested by witnesses.*

Witnesses should be present when a formal will is made by the testator. A different person would prepare the will for the testator and witnesses are required to ensure that only the intentions of the testator would be written in the will. The absence of witness would never give any effect to the will.

Each state or country requires a different number of witnesses and in the preparation of the will. The most common number is three witnesses.

- **Qualifications of a Witness**

The person designated to be a witness must meet the following qualifications:

a. He must be of legal age.

A minor, regardless of his wisdom of maturity can never qualify as a witness.

b. He must be of sound mind at the time of the making of the will.

A mentally demented person cannot become a witness in the making of a will despite being of legal age. A witness, who was cured from insanity or any temporary mental sickness, may become a witness, if he was lucid at the time of the making of the will.

A witness, who subsequently becomes mentally demented after the making of the will, would not be a ground to dishonor the will.

c. He must be able to read, write and understand the language of the will.

The primary function of the witness is to make sure that the intention of the testator prevails. There would be instances that the testator would not be familiar with the language. Thus, it is important that the witness knows and understand the language used in the preparation of the will.

d.   He must not have been convicted of any crime involving fraud;

In most countries, a person who had been convicted of a crime of falsification and fraud may not be allowed to become a witness. The aim of this rule is to erase any doubt in the preparation of the will. A person, who has a record of criminal fraud or falsification, would taint it with doubt, even if nothing evil was done during the preparation.

e.   He is not one of the direct or indirect beneficiary or heir of the testator.

A witness should not have any interest in the estate of the testator. He should not be an heir, a legatee or a devisee. In many countries, it is also required that the witness should not be related to a beneficiary, up to three degrees of consanguinity or affinity.

Therefore, a person, whose parent, son, spouse, sibling, or grandson is a legatee of the testator may not become a witness to the will.

2. If the testator chooses a different person, other than himself, to prepare the will, such person should have the same qualification as the witnesses.

The person preparing the will is also a witness to the will. Thus, he has to have the same qualification as a witness. However, he must make a separate attestation clause that he prepared the last will in testament according to how the testator wanted it.

In most cases, the person preparing the will is someone who has knowledge of the testate law, a solicitor or a notary public.

3. The witnesses and the person who prepared the will, and the testator should sign each page of the formal will.

The will may not be valid and honored if any of the signatures are missing. However, in some states, the will would still be held valid if only the participants of the will missed to sign only one page. However, a completely unsigned page of the will may invalidate the whole will or the dispositions written on the unsigned page.

4. The will should be dated and, if it exceeds one page, must be indicated with page numbers.

Just like the holographic will, formal wills should also indicate the date and the number of pages of the will. If it lacks the date or any indication as to when it was made, the will may not be deemed valid.

5. *The testator must have understood his will.*

Considering that another person prepared the will, the latter may misinterpret the intention of the testator, especially if they are writing the will in a different language. Thus, it is important that the will must be explained to the testator, so he can make necessary corrections or revisions before he signs his name.

6. There should be no alterations, revisions or additions to the written will after the same had been signed by all the parties.

Unlike the holographic will, if the testator wants to alter, remove, revise or add dispositions in his testament, he may have to revoke the previous signed will and compose a new one.

Any changes in the formal will, written in the handwriting of the testator, must again be attested by his witnesses.

However, if the testator introduced changes by adding a holographic codicil, a separate document to augment his previous will, then, he may not have it attested. Provided, however, that codicils are legally acknowledge in the country of the testator.

Example of a Formal Will

LAST WILL AND TESTAMENT

Know All Men By These Presents:

I, SAM DAVIS, an Australian Citizen, and a resident of Oakley California, of legal age, of sound mind and full understanding, and not acting under duress, force, intimidation or undue influence, do hereby execute and declare this instrument as my *last will and testament,* to wit:

Burial Rites

I wish to be buried in a tomb next to my wife, Grace Davis, under the Catholic rites.

Nomination of an Executor

I nominate and appoint my best friend, Ben Adams, a US Citizen, of legal age and a resident of Oakley, California, to be my Executor and/or personal representative of my estate, should the law allows him. Should the law disqualify him, he shall be substituted by Thomas Stern, a US Citizen, of legal age and also a resident of Oakley, California.

Taxes and Expenses

For the expenses incurred because of my illness, funeral and burial, I hereby direct my Executor to deduct the same from my account in Bank of

California, Account 123456789. Provided however, it shall not exceed $10,000.

For the payment of the taxes of my estate, I hereby direct my executor to sell my beach house, located in #26 4th Avenue, Orange County, California.

Should the property be not sufficient to pay for my taxes, I hereby direct that the remaining amount shall be paid using the bank account stated in the previous paragraph.

Institution of Heir

I hereby institute my son, Alex Davis, a US Citizen, of legal age and a resident of Oakley, California, to be my only legal heir. All of my estate that had not been distributed, rights that had not been waived, and obligation that had not been fulfilled, shall be owned and fulfilled by him.

Disposition of Property

I hereby dispose my property, real or personal, wherever they may be situated and subject to the limitation prescribed by the law, as follows:

1. To my son, Harrison Davis, I give and bequeath all my cars existing at the time of my death;

2. To my daughter, Anna Davis-Jones, I give and bequeath my residence situated in #34,

Rose St., Oakley, California, including all the furniture and decorations existing until my death;

3. To my grandson, Louis Davis Jones, I hereby direct my executor to set up a trust fund in his name in the amount of $300,000.00, with the Bank of California, which would be held in trust until he reached the age of 21.

4. To my best friend, Steven Michaels, I hereby give and bequeath my collection of watches, stored in the Bank of California. Provided however, that should he choose to sell them, he shall give first preference to my children as buyers.

Rights and Obligations

I hereby grant or revoke the rights, or waive my rights to the following persons, natural or juridical, to wit:

1. To my tenant, Chelsea Trump, who occupies room 1006 in the tenth floor of the Clinton Tower, in 134 Avenue, New York, New York, I hereby waive my rights to any back rentals, she had;

2. To my tenant, Melanie Mitchell, I hereby grant her the rights to occupy the biggest

room in the seventh floor of the Clinton tower, for two years, without any rental;

3. To my tenant, Jack Barrack, I hereby revoke his right to renew his contract of lease over the commercial space in the second floor of Clinton Tower;

Revocation of Previous Will*

I hereby declare that my previous will, made and signed on March 2, 2012, and all the testamentary dispositions written therein, REVOKED and ineffective.

I HEREBY SAYETH NONE.

In view thereof, I have set my hand this June 24, 2017 in the City of Oakley California.

Signed, Sam Davis

WITNESS ATTESTATION CLAUSE

We, Doris Bay and Franklin Webb, US Citizen and resident of Oakley California, after having been sworn to in accordance with law**, hereby depose and say:

1. That we personally know Sam Davis as a US Citizen and a resident of Oakley California;

2. That he had caused the making of his last will and testament through Ron Davidson, a notary public in the State of California;

3. That we hereby attest that Sam Davis understood the language and contents of the will and affixed his signature voluntarily.

4. That we have read and understood the same instrument before Sam Davis affixed his signature;

5. That we hereby attest that the words in the last will and testament convey all the intentions of the testator.

6. That we hereby guarantee that we are one of the beneficiaries, or related to any of the beneficiary within the third degree.

Affiant sayeth none.

Signed: The Doris Bay and Franklin Webb

AFFIDAVIT OF THE MAKER***

I, Regan Martin, US Citizen, and a resident of Oakley California, after having been duly sworn to in accordance with law, do hereby state and declare:

1. That I personally know Sam Davis, the testator for this last will and testament
2. That I prepared this instrument in accordance to his wishes and pursuant to the existing laws on succession and inheritance;
3. That all the dispositions herein are of his own choice and free will; no third person influenced, forced or intimidated him to make the dispositions and to sign the instrument;
4. That the will is written in a language known and understand by him and the witnesses;
5. That the instrument was read by him and the witnesses.

Affiant sayeth none.

ACKNOWLEDGEMENT****

Before me, a notary public for the city of Oakley California, this 24th day of June 2017. The testator, the person who prepared his will and his witnesses personally appeared before me, with their valid Social Service Identification, a machine copy of which is hereto attached.

The said persons are known to me as the persons who executed the respective instruments and acknowledged to me that the same is of their own voluntary will and act.

The testator and his witnesses all signed above their name and at the left margin of every page.

This last will and testament consists three pages including the attestations and this acknowledgement.

IN WITNESS WHEREOF, I have hereunto affixed my signature and the seal granted to me by the state.

Notary public
Description or expiration of his license

*If the testator had made a previous will, he should indicate whether he is revoking it. If he failed to do so, all the dispositions in the previous will would remain valid, unless it is in conflict with the new will.

**If the will is notarial will, then the phrase "after being sworn to in accordance with law" needs to be stated.

*** An additional attestation by the person who prepared the will is necessary if the person who prepared the will is neither the testator nor the notary public.

**** Only necessary if you opt for a notarial will.

Chapter Five: Writing Testamentary Dispositions

The three things that a testator could put in his testamentary dispositions are discussed in Chapter One. These are the properties, rights and obligation of the testator. This chapter would discuss what properties, rights, and obligations may be disposed by the testator and what could affect their validity.

Disposing Properties in Your Will
When writing the testamentary disposition over a property, words like "Give", "Award" and "Bequeath" or any words with the same meaning, must be included. Without these words, the provision may become questionable.

• *Examples of a proper and accepted testamentary disposition of a property:*

> To Ben James, I give and bequeath 8 of my cars, herein described as follows: (Descriptions of the cars.)
>
> To Thomas Henry, I give and bequeath my mansion in Beverly Hills, specifically located at (Complete address of the

> I give and bequeath:
>
> • To Ben James, 8 cars (Followed with the descriptions.)
>
> • To Thomas Henry, a mansion in Beverly Hills. (Followed with the exact address

The second example is known as a collective disposition. The heirs, legatees or devisees mentioned and the properties bequeathed to them may be enumerated after the phrase denoting the bequeathing.

However, there should not be an interruption in the enumeration. Any interruption may cause ambiguity to the will.

Example:

> I give and bequeath:
>
> • To Ben James, 8 cars (Followed with the descriptions.)
>
> Note to the executor: Please instruct Ben to take care of all of them.
>
> • To Thomas Henry, a mansion in Beverly Hills. (Followed with the exact address

Here, some of the heirs may question the provision about Thomas Henry. It would not be clear if the

Thomas is to receive the mansion, or if he only has to take care of it.

- *Examples of a vague testamentary disposition of a property:*

My Last Will and Testament
To Ben James, 8 cars (Followed with the descriptions.)
To Thomas Henry, a mansion in Beverly Hills. (Followed with the exact address

- This is vague and unacceptable because there is no indication as to the real intention of the testator. This may be cured or can be totally declared invalid.

Properties that Can Be Disposed

- All properties, tangible or intangible, living or not living, owned by the testator can be subject of a testamentary disposition, regardless of their status and provided that they are not illegal.

Examples of dispositions that are considered illegal:

a. Bequeathing an unlicensed and prohibited guns;

b. Bequeathing the proceeds of a sale from prohibited drugs;
   c. Giving personal properties that were declared stolen;

- A property that is encumbered, mortgage, or protested, can be bequeathed by the testator. However, the title should still be in the name of the testator, at the time of the making of the will.

Question:

Sam mortgaged his Beverly Hills mansion to the Bank of California. In his will, he gave the mansion to his friend, Thomas. A few days after he died, the Bank of California foreclosed the property. Is the disposition valid?

Answer:

The disposition is valid. Sam is still the owner of the property at the time he made the will. He had all the rights over the property. However, whether the disposition can be executed or not, is a different situation.

Here, the disposition is likely to be dishonored.

- Future properties can become a subject of a disposition if the process of acquiring such properties began at the time of the making of the will. Properties the testator wished or opted to buy, but failed to acquire while he is still alive cannot be a subject of a testamentary disposition.

Question:

Sam was in the process of buying property in Charlotte, North Carolina. He already paid for the down payment, but the title was yet to be transferred to him. He gave this property to Ben James in his will. Is the testamentary disposition valid?

Answer:

Yes. Sam paid the down payment. He has an interest of ownership over the property.

The property owner, in most cases, is required to demand for the fulfillment of the contract. If he refuses, Ben can demand the executor of the will to demand the fulfillment of the contract.

Question No. 2:

How about in the previous example, Sam did not pay the down payment. Instead, he only paid an "option" money. Is the testamentary disposition valid?

Answer:

In this situation, the disposition is not valid. Option money does not give Sam an interest of ownership.

Thus, he had no right to dispose the property. The property owner also has no right to demand the fulfillment of the contract.

*In sales, option money is a reservation payment, so the owner will not sell it to other buyers at a specific period.

Granting and Revoking Rights

Words like "grant", "bestow", and "award" may indicate that a right is being given to an heir, legatee or devisee. A testator should clearly declare his intention to bestow a right through these words to avoid confusion.

The testator may also revoke rights he gave during his lifetime through his will. These provisions are often indicated by the words, "REVOKE" and "PROHIBIT"

Examples of a Proper Way to Bestow and Revoke Rights in the Will:

> To Ben, I hereby grant him the right to occupy my farm, (followed by the address and description) for two years, for free, provided that he should be liable for the taxes over the land.
>
> To Henry, I award him a scholarship to any of the universities he may qualify as a student.
>
> As to Thomas, I hereby REVOKE all his rights as a free member of the ABC Finance Club.

Rights that can be granted in the Will

➢ The general rule is that all rights that can be waived during the lifetime of the testator may also be granted by him in his will. These rights usually affect the liberty of the testator.

Examples of the rights that may be waived are:

1. The right of membership to an elite club;
2. The right to refuse rental fees for a leased property;
3. Rights to bring civil actions against someone;

Rights that may not be granted are usually the rights solely given by the constitution to the testator, such as the right to suffrage.

➢ **Filial Rights**

Filial rights may be bestowed by the testator by acknowledging his blood relationship to another person, who may or may not be one of the named heirs in his will

By doing so, he may have entitled that relative to some rights over his estate.

Rights that can be revoked in the Will

The general rule is that all rights waived by the testator during his lifetime may be revoked by him, through his will, except the following:

a. Rights that are anchored with interest;

Question:

Sam revoked the contract of lease executed by him in favor of Ben in his will. The contract of lease was for a period of 5 years. Upon Sam's death, there was still two years left in the contract. Can Sam's revocation be given effect?

Answer:

No, because the right given to Ben was anchored with interest. Ben was legally entitled because of the contract. The contract could not be rescinded solely by the testator.

b. Rights granted specifically by laws.

Question:

The state recognizes the rights of compulsory heirs. Sam did not want to give the right to inherit to Ben, so he revoked his right by writing, "I revoked Ben's right to inherit as one of my compulsory heirs." Is this testamentary provision acceptable?

Answer:

No. The right is granted by law to Ben. Sam has no power over such right. However, he can disinherit Ben.

Disinheriting an Heir

One of the advantages of having a will is to disinherit a compulsory heir. This right allows the testator to not give any of his estate to an heir who disrespected, threatened, or abandoned him. Disinheritance is only common to states which grant rights to compulsory heirs to inherit a designated portion of the estate.

However, disinheriting an heir can endanger the validity of the will. A wrongful disinheritance of a compulsory heir may result to preterition. When a compulsory heir is not given his due inheritance, he can protest the will and have it declared void for violating a law.

The right of the testator to disinherit an heir in his will must conform to the provisions of law. In most countries, an heir may only be disinherited if he commits the following act of ingratitude:

1. He attempted to commit a grave crime against the person of the testator or any of the immediate family of the latter.

Example: Sam is Ben's son. When Ben remarried, Sam attempted to murder Ben's new wife. If Ben disinherits Sam, citing the attempted murder, the disinheritance is justified and valid.

However, if Sam killed his new stepbrother, Ben might not disinherit Sam because he did not commit a crime to Ben's immediate family.

2. He abandoned the testator at a time the latter needed support. This is subjective.

Question:

Sam and Ben are brothers. Sam refused to support Ben when the latter was paralyzed and not able to feed and care for himself.

Luckily, Ben got better and won millions in lottery. He harbored ill feeling to Sam, so he decided to disinherit him, citing the abandonment as a ground. Is this valid?

Answer:

Yes. Sam's abandonment is a proof that he severed his family ties with Ben. He did not consider the latter as his brother, and thus, abandoned his right as a brother and compulsory heir to Ben.

However, the disinheritance may be void, if Sam's abandonment is justified because he also did not have the capability to support Ben.

3. The compulsory heir squandered or defrauded the testator.

Defrauding the testator is a grave act of disrespect. In many countries, when an immediate family defrauds another, the crime is often pardoned to avoid severing family ties. The testator may use it as a ground to disinherit a compulsory heir.

For example: Ben defrauded Sam in the amount of $50,000. In his will, Sam disinherited Ben, citing the crime as the ground. This is deemed valid.

In disinheriting a compulsory heir, the testator should always indicate it with the word "DISINHERIT". The absence of this word may invalidate the disinheritance for ambiguity.

Disposing Obligations

A disposition of obligations can be written depending on the type of obligation. These are the pure obligations and conditional obligations.

Pure Obligation

A pure obligation, which does not have any conditions, may be indicated with the words

"DEMAND and OBLIGE". Pure obligations are often directed to the executor or the instituted heir because they will be the one to do the physical demand of the obligation.

Examples on how to write provision for a pure obligation in the will

> I DEMAND Ben to pay me the $3000, I loaned to him on February 7, 2010 within three months upon my death. I hereby DIRECT my executor to do all the necessary process to ensure the fulfillment thereof.

Conditional Obligations

Conditional obligations, as mentioned before, are anchored to another disposition. It is often denoted by the words, "PROVIDED" or "BUT WITH THE CONDITION" or "ONLY AFTER (or WHEN, IF)

Example of a Testamentary Disposition with Condition

> To Sam Jones, I give and bequeath my mansion in Palm Spring, (complete address), provided he qualifies as a Harvard Law Student.
>
> To Ben James, I give and bequeath $20,000, but with the condition that he would use it to open a business.
>
> To Thomas Henry, I give and bequeath my shares to ABC Corporation, only after, he graduates from college.

- **Valid Conditions**

If the main disposition is void, the conditional obligation is also declared void. A void condition, however, will not declare the disposition void. It would still take effect without the need to fulfill the condition.

The conditions can be as simple or as complicated, depending on the testator, provided there is a probability or possibility that it could happen.

Examples of Valid conditions:

1. If it rains on June 4, 2015;
2. When he becomes a doctor
3. If he gives birth to twins.

*If there is no period given, it meant during the lifetime of the heir.

- **Invalid Conditions**

Improbable and impossible conditions are invalid conditions. Improbable conditions are those that may never happen, such as the sun rising on the west.

A condition may be impossible for the following reasons:

1. The object of the condition is destroyed or inexistent;

Example: Sam gave Ben a condition to marry his daughter Michelle. However, Michelle died a day before Sam died. The condition, therefore, became inexistent.

2. The condition is to do something illegal;

Example: Sam gave and bequeathed $10 million cash to Ben, only if Ben would kill ten people.

The condition is deemed impossible for being illegal.

3. The condition is to make a testator the instituted heir of the receiving heir. This is known as a disposition *captatoria.*

Example: Sam would give three acres of farmland to Ben situated in Wyoming, provided that Ben should also execute a will, naming Sam as his heir.

4. The condition prohibits the heir to use and dispose the property during the latter's life time.

Example: Sam gave his son, Ben, a diamond-crusted Rolex watch. However, he added a condition prohibiting Ben to sell, donate, or to dispose the watch as long as Ben lives.

This condition is impossible. It would appear that Ben had never inherited anything.

- **Effects of Invalid Conditions**

An invalid condition will not render the testamentary disposition void. The disposition would only be viewed by the executor or by the courts like it had no conditions at all.

A valid condition, however, would be rendered void if the testamentary disposition itself is declared void.

Example of a valid testamentary disposition with invalid condition:

> Sam would give Thomas the BMV car upon his death if the latter kills Sam's wife.
>
> Since the condition is invalid, Thomas would receive the BMV without the need to fulfill the condition.

Example of a void Testamentary disposition with valid condition

Sam gave and bequeathed Thomas his neighbors BMV car if it rains on the day of his funeral.

Thomas would not get the BMV car even if it rains on the day of Sam's funeral because the disposition is impossible and void.

Chapter 6: Revocation, Destruction and Execution of the Will

Disposing the Property Subject of the Will

Some people refuse to make a will at a younger age because of a misconception. They think that when a property becomes a subject of the will, it could no longer be disturbed or disposed.

A will only grants inchoate rights to the heirs. They do not get any rights to the property until the testator dies. Thus, the testator could still dispose his property, which is a subject of a testamentary disposition.

If the testator had disposed the property, the testamentary disposition would still be valid, but it cannot only be executed.

Revocation of the Will

Revocation of the will can happen because of the following:

1. The testator no longer intends to leave a will.

The testator could either execute another instrument revoking his will or he could destroy the will.

2. The testator wants to change all or a portion of his will.

The testator may make a new will, containing the new provisions. But, he must indicate in a separate paragraph a declaration of revoking his previous wills. (See the example of Formal Will in Chapter Four)

If the testator fails to make the declaration, then both of his will would be recognized. If conflicts arise between the old and new dispositions, the new one would be recognized.

Destruction of the Will

The destruction of the will do not make it lose its effect. That is the general rule. But, if the testator destroys his will with the intention to revoke or rid it with effect, then the destruction would be tantamount to a valid revocation.

Codicils and Altering the Original Will without Making a New One

A testator is not prohibited from altering his original will. However, he must do it according to the law and procedure observed by his state or in effect during the making of his will.

One way of adding new or revoking dispositions is to add a codicil. A codicil is a supplementary instrument that augments, clarifies or revoke testamentary dispositions in the original will.

Validity of Codicil

A codicil takes the same form as the will. If the original will is a holographic will, the codicil must also be completely written in the handwriting of the testator.

A formal codicil requires the same formalities as the formal will, but with fewer witnesses and without the need of a participation of a notary public.

In some cases, a formal will may be altered through the execution of a holographic codicil.

Execution of the Will

The execution of the will is directed to an executor. Every state has different qualifications for an executor. Here are some of the most common qualifications:

1. He must be of legal age;

2. He must be a citizen of the state where the will was made. If the will was made in New York, the executor must be an American citizen.

3. The executor has not been convicted of any crime of fraud. In some states, a felon could never be an executor;

4. The executor can read and write and understands the language of the will;

It should be noted that, unlike the witnesses to a will, an executor may be an heir or a beneficiary of the will.

The instituted heir may act as an executor, in the absence of the nomination of executor or if the nominee failed to qualify. If there are many instituted heir, then the probate court may choose the executor.

Probate of the Will

The will can be executed upon the qualification of the executor, unless the governing law requires that the will has to be probated.

Probate is the process for which the formalities of the will are examined. The jurisdiction of the probate court is only limited to the extrinsic validity of the will.

If the Probate court declares the will to be complete in form, then it would direct the executor to continue with the execution of the provisions.

Any questions about the intrinsic or substantive validity of the will or the disposition should be brought separately before the inheritance court, if one is designated in the state.

Who Can Bring the Will for Probate?

The following person can bring the will for probate before the courts:

1. The testator himself;

    The testator may opt to avoid disputes after his death and may choose to have his will probated prior to his death.

2. The executor; or in the absence thereof

3. The sole instituted heir;

4. The eldest child or heir of the testator, if there are two or more instituted heir.

Effect if the Will is Declared Invalid by the Probate Court

When it is the testator who caused the will to be probated, he may execute another will that would meet the formalities and would be approved by the probate court.

When the will is declared void by the probate court or inheritance court, after the death of the testator, the testamentary succession will not be observed. Intestate succession would take over.

Conclusion

Thank you again for purchasing this book.

I hope that this book had given you an overview about testamentary succession. Now, that you know about what should be included in your last will and testament, and how it should be done, I encourage you to make your will as soon as possible.

Do not let your family be ripped apart because of disputes about your property. Even if you only own a few properties, it would make a difference upon your death. Thus, make sure to settle things for your heirs.

I also encourage you to have this book read by your family or your friends, so they would know their own rights.

Made in the USA
Lexington, KY
17 June 2019